DATE DUE

EDMOND

Edmond

A Play by

David Mamet

Grove Press, Inc./New York

GROVE PRESS, INC., 196 West Houston Street, New York, N.Y. 10014

To Richard Nelson and Wally Shawn

The world premiere of *Edmond* was produced by the Goodman Theatre, Chicago, Illinois, June 4, 1982, with the following cast:

Paul Butler	A Mission Preacher, A Prisoner
Rick Cluchey	The Manager, A Leafleteer, A Customer, A Policeman, A Guard
Joyce Hazard	A B-Girl, A Whore
Laura Innes	A Peep Show Girl, Glenna
Bruce Jarchow	A Man in a Bar, A Hotel Clerk, The Man in Back, A Chaplain
Linda Kimbrough	Edmond's Wife
Marge Kotlisky	The Fortune-teller, A Manager, A Woman in the Subway
Ernest Perry, Jr.	A Shill, A Pimp
José Santana	A Cardsharp, A Guard
Colin Stinton	Edmond
Jack Wallace	A Bartender, A Bystander, A Pawnshop Owner, An Interrogator

This production was directed by Gregory Mosher; settings by Bill Bartelt; lighting by Kevin Rigdon; costumes by Marsha Kowal, fight choreography by David Woolley; stage managers, Tom Biscotto and Anne Clarke.

The New York production opened at the Provincetown Playhouse on October 27, 1982, with Lionel Mark Smith playing the roles of A SHILL, A PIMP.

Hokey Pokey Wickey Wamm
Salacapinkus Muley Comm
Tamsey Wamsey Wierey Wamm
King of the Cannibal Islands

—*Popular Song*

The Characters

FORTUNE-TELLER
EDMOND, a man in his mid thirties
HIS WIFE
A MAN IN A BAR
A B-GIRL
A BARTENDER
THE MANAGER
A PEEP-SHOW GIRL
THREE GAMBLERS
A CARD SHARP
A BYSTANDER
TWO SHILLS
A LEAFLETEER
A MANAGER (F)
A WHORE
A HOTEL CLERK
A PAWNSHOP OWNER
A CUSTOMER
THE MAN IN BACK
A WOMAN ON THE SUBWAY
A PIMP
GLENNA, a waitress
A TRAMP

A MISSION PREACHER
A POLICEMAN
AN INTERROGATOR
A PRISONER
A CHAPLAIN
A GUARD

The Setting

New York City

Scene One
The Fortune-Teller

EDMOND *and the* **FORTUNE-TELLER** *seated across the table from each other.*

FORTUNE-TELLER: If things are predetermined surely they must manifest themselves.
When we look back—as we look back—we see that we could never have done otherwise than as we did. *(Pause.)*
Surely, then, there must have been signs.
If only we could have read them.
We say, "I see now that I could not have done otherwise . . . my *diet* caused me. Or my stars . . . which caused me to eat what I ate . . . or my *genes*, or some other thing beyond my control forced me to act as I did. . . ."
And those things which *forced* us, of course, must make their signs: our *diet*, or our *genes*, or our *stars*.

(Pause.)
And there *are* signs. *(Pause.)*
What we see reflects (more than what is) what is to be. *(Pause.)*
Are you cold?

EDMOND: No. *(Pause.)*

FORTUNE-TELLER: Would you like me to close the window?

EDMOND: No, thank you.

FORTUNE-TELLER: Give me your palm.

(EDMOND *does so.)*

You are not where you belong. It is perhaps true none of us are, but in your case this is more true than in most. We all like to believe we are special. In your case this is true.
Listen to me. *(She continues talking as the lights dim.)* The world seems to be crumbling around us. You look and you wonder if what you perceive is accurate. And you are unsure what your place is. To what extent you are cause and to what an effect. . . .

Scene Two.
At Home.

EDMOND *and his* WIFE *are sitting in the living room. A pause.*

WIFE: The girl broke the lamp. *(Pause.)*

EDMOND: Which lamp?

WIFE: The antique lamp.

EDMOND: In my room?

WIFE: Yes. *(Pause.)*

EDMOND: Huh.

WIFE: That lamp cost over two hundred and twenty dollars.

EDMOND *(Pause):* Maybe we can get it fixed.

WIFE: We're never going to get it fixed,
I think that that's the *point.* . . .
I think that's why she did it.

EDMOND: Yes. Alright—I'm going.

(Pause. He gets up and starts out of the room.)

WIFE: Will you bring me back some cigarettes. . . .

EDMOND: I'm not coming back.

WIFE: What?

EDMOND: I'm not coming back. *(Pause.)*

WIFE: What do you mean?

EDMOND: I'm going, and I'm not going to come back. *(Pause.)*

WIFE: You're not *ever* coming back?

EDMOND: No.

WIFE: Why not? *(Pause.)*

EDMOND: I don't want to live this kind of life.

WIFE: What does that mean?

EDMOND: That I can't live this life.

WIFE: "You can't live this life" so you're leaving me.

EDMOND: Yes.

WIFE: Ah. Ah. Ah.
And what about *ME?*
Don't you *love* me anymore?

EDMOND: No.

WIFE: You don't.

EDMOND: No.

WIFE: And why is that?

EDMOND: I don't know.

WIFE: And when did you find this out?

EDMOND: A long time ago.

WIFE: You did.

EDMOND: Yes.

WIFE: How long ago?

EDMOND: Years ago.

WIFE: You've known for years that you don't love me.

EDMOND: Yes. *(Pause.)*

WIFE: Oh. *(Pause.)* Then why did you decide you're leaving *now?*

EDMOND: I've had enough.

WIFE: Yes. But why *now?*

EDMOND *(pause):* Because you don't interest me spiritually or sexually. *(Pause.)*

WIFE: Hadn't you known this for some time?

EDMOND: What do you think?

WIFE: I think you did.

EDMOND: Yes, I did.

WIFE: And why didn't you leave *then?*
Why didn't you leave *then,* you stupid *shit!!!*
All of these years you say that you've been living
here? . . . *(Pause.)*
Eh? You idiot. . . .
I've had enough.
You idiot . . . to see you passing *judgment* on me all
this time . . .

EDMOND: . . . I never judged you. . . .

WIFE: . . . and then you tell me. "You're leaving."

EDMOND: Yes.

WIFE: *Go,* then. . . .

EDMOND: I'll call you.

WIFE: Please. And we'll talk. What shall we do with
the house? Cut it in half?
Go. Get out of here. Go.

EDMOND: You think that I'm fooling.

WIFE: I do *not.* Good-bye. Thank you. Good-bye.
(Pause.) Good-bye. *(Pause.)*
Get *out.* Get *out* of here.
And don't you *ever* come back.
Do you hear me?

(WIFE *exits. Closing the door on him.)*

Scene Three.
A Bar.

EDMOND *is at the bar. A* **MAN** *is next to him. They sit for a while.*

MAN: . . . I'll tell you who's got it *easy*. . . .

EDMOND: Who?

MAN: The niggers. *(Pause.)* Sometimes I wish I was a nigger.

EDMOND: Sometimes I do, too.

MAN: I'd rob a store. I don't blame them.
I swear to God. Because I want to tell you: we're *bred* to do the things that we do.

EDMOND: Mm.

MAN: Northern races *one* thing, and the southern races something else. And what *they* want to do is sit beneath the tree and watch the elephant. *(Pause.)* And I don't blame them one small bit. Because there's too much *pressure* on us.

EDMOND: Yes.

MAN: And that's no joke, and that's not *poetry*, it's just too much.

EDMOND: It is. It absolutely is.

MAN: A man's got to get *out*. . . .

EDMOND: What do you mean?

MAN: A man's got to get *away* from himself. . . .

EDMOND: . . . that's true . . .

MAN: . . . because the pressure is too much.

EDMOND: What do you do?

MAN: What do you mean?

EDMOND: What do you do to get out?

MAN: What do I do?

EDMOND: Yes.

MAN: What are the things to do? What are the things *anyone* does? . . . *(Pause.)*
Pussy . . . I don't know. . . . *Pussy* . . . *Power* . . .
Money . . . uh . . . *adventure* . . . *(Pause.)*
I think that's it . . . uh, self-*destruction*. . .
I think that that's it . . . don't you? . . .

EDMOND: Yes.

MAN: . . . uh, *religion* . . . I suppose that's it, uh, *release*, uh, ratification. *(Pause.)*

You have to get *out*, you have to get something opens your *nose*, life is too short.

EDMOND: My wife and I are incompatible.

MAN: I'm sorry to hear that. *(Pause.)*
In what way?

EDMOND: I don't find her attractive.

MAN: Mm.

EDMOND: It's a boring thing to talk about. But that's what's on my mind.

MAN: I understand.

EDMOND: You do?

MAN: Yes. *(Pause.)*

EDMOND: Thank you.

MAN: Believe me, that's alright. I know that we all *need* it, and we don't know where to *get* it, and I know what it *means*, and I understand.

EDMOND: . . . I feel . . .

MAN: I know. Like your balls were cut off.

EDMOND: Yes. A long, long time ago.

MAN: Mm-hm.

EDMOND: And I don't feel like a man.

MAN: Do you know what you need?

EDMOND: No.

MAN: You need to get laid.

EDMOND: I do. I know I do.

MAN: That's why the niggers have it easy.

EDMOND: Why?

MAN: I'll tell you why: there are responsibilities they never have accepted. *(Pause.)*
Try the Allegro.

EDMOND: What is that?

MAN: A bar on Forty-seventh Street.

EDMOND: Thank you.

(The MAN gets up, pays for drinks.)

MAN: I want this to be on me. I want you to *remember* there was someone who listened. *(Pause.)*
You'd do the same for me.

(The MAN exits.)

Scene Four.
The Allegro

EDMOND *sits by himself for a minute. A* **B-GIRL** *comes by.*

B-GIRL: You want to buy me a drink?

EDMOND: Yes. *(Pause.)*
I'm putting myself at your *mercy* . . . this is my first time in a place like this. I don't want to be taken advantage of. *(Pause.)*
You understand?

B-GIRL: Buy me a drink and we'll go in the back.

EDMOND: And do what?

B-GIRL: Whatever you want.

(**EDMOND** *leans over and whispers to* **B-GIRL**.)

B-GIRL: Ten dollars.

EDMOND: Alright.

B-GIRL: Buy me a drink.

EDMOND: You get a commission on the drinks?

B-GIRL: Yes.

(She gestures to **BARTENDER,** *who brings drinks.)*

EDMOND: How much commission do you get?

B-GIRL: Fifty percent.

BARTENDER *(bringing drinks):* That's twenty bucks.

EDMOND *(getting up):* It's too much.

BARTENDER: What?

EDMOND: Too much. Thank you.

B-GIRL: Ten!

EDMOND: No, thank you.

B-GIRL: Ten!

EDMOND: I'll give you five. I'll give you the five you'd get for the drink if I gave them ten. But I'm not going to give them ten.

B-GIRL: But you have to buy me a drink.

EDMOND: I'm sorry. No.

B-GIRL: Alright. *(Pause.)* Give me ten.

EDMOND: On top of the ten?

B-GIRL: Yeah. You give me twenty.

EDMOND: I should give you twenty.

B-GIRL: Yes.

EDMOND: To *you.*

B-GIRL: Yes.

EDMOND: And then you give him the five?

B-GIRL: Yes. I got to give him the five.

EDMOND: No.

B-GIRL: For the *drink.*

EDMOND: No. You don't have to pay him for the drink. It's *tea* . . .

B-GIRL: It's not tea.

EDMOND: It's not tea!? . . .

(He drinks.)

If it's not *tea* what *is* it, then? . . .
I came here to be *straight* with you, why do we have to go *through* this? . . .

MANAGER: Get in or get out. *(Pause.)*
Don't mill around.
Get in or get out . . . *(Pause.)*
Alright.

*(**MANAGER** escorts **EDMOND** out of the bar.)*

Scene Five

A Peep Show.

Booths with closed doors all around. A **GIRL** *in a spangled leotard sees* **EDMOND** *and motions him to a booth whose door she is opening.*

GIRL: Seven. Go in Seven.

(He starts to Booth Seven.)

No. Six! I mean Six. Go in Six.

(He goes into Booth Six. She disappears behind the row of booths, and appears behind a plexiglass partition in Booth Six.)

Take your dick out. *(Pause.)*
Take your dick out. *(Pause.)*
Come on. Take your dick out.

EDMOND: I'm not a cop.

GIRL: I know you're not a cop. Take your dick out. I'm gonna give you a good time.

EDMOND: How can we get this barrier to come down?

GIRL: It doesn't come down.

EDMOND: Then how are you going to give me a good time?

GIRL: Come here.

(He leans close. She whispers.)

Give me ten bucks. *(Pause.)*
Give me ten bucks. *(Pause.)*
Put it through the thing.

(She indicates a small ventilator hole in the plexiglass. Pause.)

Put it through the thing.

EDMOND   *(checking his wallet):*   I haven't got ten bucks.

GIRL: Okay . . . just . . . yes.
Okay. Give me the twenty.

EDMOND: Are you going to give me change?

GIRL: Yes. Just give me the twenty. Give it to me. Good. Now take your dick out.

EDMOND: Can I have my ten?

GIRL: Look. Let me hold the ten.

EDMOND: Give me my ten back. *(Pause.)*
Come on. Give me my ten back.

GIRL: Let me hold the ten. . . .

EDMOND: Give me my ten back and I'll give you a tip when you're done.

(Pause. She does so.)
Thank you.

GIRL: Okay. Take your dick out.

EDMOND *(of the plexiglass):* How does this thing come down?

GIRL: It doesn't come down.

EDMOND: It doesn't come down?

GIRL: No.

EDMOND: Then what the fuck am I giving you ten bucks for?

GIRL: Look: You can touch me. Stick your finger in this you can touch me.

EDMOND: I don't want to touch *you*. . . .
I want *you* to touch *me*. . . .

GIRL: I can't. *(Pause.)* I would, but I can't. We'd have the cops in here. We would.
Honestly. *(Pause.)*
Look: Put your finger in here . . . come on.
(Pause.) Come on.

(He zips his pants up and leaves the booth.)

You're only cheating your*self*. . . .

Scene Six.

On the Street. Three-Card Monte.

A CARDSHARP, a BYSTANDER and TWO SHILLS.

SHARPER: You pick the red you win, and twenty get
you forty. Put your money up.
The *black* gets *back*, the *red* you go ahead. . . .
Who saw the red? . . . Who saw the red?
Who saw her? . . .

BYSTANDER *(to* EDMOND):   The fellow over there
is a shill . . .

EDMOND: Who is? . . .

BYSTANDER *(points):*   You want to know how to beat
the game?

EDMOND: How?

BYSTANDER: You figure out which card has *got* to
win. . . .

EDMOND: . . . Uh-huh . . .

BYSTANDER: . . . and bet the *other* one.

SHARPER: Who saw the Red? . . .

BYSTANDER: They're all shills, they're all part of an act.

SHARPER: Who saw her? Five will get you ten. . . .

SHILL: *(playing lookout):* Cops . . . cops . . . cops . . . *don't* run . . . *don't* run. . . .

(Everyone scatters. **EDMOND** *moves down the street.)*

Scene Seven.
Passing Out Leaflets.

EDMOND *moves down the street. A man is passing out leaflets.*

LEAFLETEER: Check it out . . . check it out. . . . This˙is what you looking for. . . . Take it . . . I'm *giving* you something. . . . *Take* it. . . .

(EDMOND *takes the leaflet.)*

Now: Is that what you looking for or not? . . .

EDMOND *(reading the leaflet):*   Is this true? . . .

LEAFLETEER: Would I give it to you if it wasn't? . . .

(EDMOND *walks off reading the leaflet. The* **LEAFLETEER** *continues with his spiel.)*

Check it out. . . .

Scene Eight.
The Whorehouse.

EDMOND *shows up with the leaflet. He talks to the* **MANAGER,** *a woman.*

MANAGER: Hello.

EDMOND: Hello.

MANAGER: Have you been here before?

EDMOND: No.

MANAGER: How'd you hear about us? (**EDMOND** *shows her the leaflet.)* You from out of town?

EDMOND: Yes. What's the deal here?

MANAGER: This is a *health* club.

EDMOND: . . . I know.

MANAGER: And our rates are by the hour. *(Pause.)*

EDMOND: Yes?

MANAGER: Sixty-eight dollars for the first hour, sauna, free bar, showers . . . *(Pause.)*
The hour doesn't start until you and the masseuse are in the room.

EDMOND: Alright.

MANAGER: Whatever happens in the room, of course, is between you.

EDMOND: I understand.

MANAGER: You understand?

EDMOND: Yes.

MANAGER: . . . Or, for two hours it's one hundred fifty dollars. If you want two hostesses that is two hundred dollars for one hour. *(Pause.)* Whatever arrangement that you choose to make with *them* is between *you.*

EDMOND: Good. *(Pause.)*

MANAGER: What would you like?

EDMOND: One hour.

MANAGER: You pay that now. How would you like to pay?

EDMOND: How can I pay?

MANAGER: With cash or credit card. The billing for the card will read "Atlantic Ski and Tennis."

EDMOND: I'll pay you with cash.

Scene Nine.
Upstairs At The Whorehouse.

EDMOND *and the* **WHORE** *are in a cubicle.*

WHORE: How are you?

EDMOND: Fine. I've never done this before.

WHORE: No?

(She starts rubbing his neck.)

EDMOND: No. That feels very good. *(Pause.)*

WHORE: You've got a good body.

EDMOND: Thank you.

WHORE: Do you work out? *(Pause.)*

EDMOND: I jog.

WHORE: Mmm. *(Pause.)*

EDMOND: And I used to play football in high school.

WHORE: You've kept yourself in good shape.

EDMOND: Thank you.

WHORE *(pause):* What shall we do?

EDMOND: I'd like to have intercourse with you.

WHORE: That sounds very nice. I'd like that, too.

EDMOND: You would?

WHORE: Yes.

EDMOND: How much would that be?

WHORE: For a straight fuck, that would be a hundred fifty.

EDMOND: That's too much.

WHORE: You know that I'm giving you a break. . . .

EDMOND: . . . no . . .

WHORE: . . . Because this is your first time here. . . .

EDMOND: No. It's too much, on top of the sixty-eight at the door. . . .

WHORE: . . . I know, I know, but you know, I don't get to keep it all. I *split* it with them. Yes. They don't pay me, I pay *them*.

EDMOND: It's too much. *(Pause. The* **WHORE** *sighs.)*

WHORE: How much do you have?

EDMOND: All I had was one hundred for the whole thing.

WHORE: You mean a hundred for it all.

EDMOND: That only left me thirty.

WHORE: Noooo, honey, you couldn't get a *thing* for that.

EDMOND: Well, how much do you want?

WHORE *(sighs):* Alright, for a straight fuck, one hundred twenty.

EDMOND: I couldn't pay that.

WHORE: I'm sorry, then. It would have been nice.

EDMOND: I'll give you eighty.

WHORE: No.

EDMOND: One hundred.

WHORE: Alright, but only, you know, 'cause this is your first time.

EDMOND: I know.

WHORE: . . . 'cause we *split* with them, you understand. . . .

EDMOND: I understand.

WHORE: Alright. One hundred.

EDMOND: Thank you. I appreciate this. *(Pause.)* Would it offend you if I wore a rubber? . . .

WHORE: Not at all. *(Pause.)*

EDMOND: Do you have one? . . .

WHORE: Yes. *(Pause.)* You want to pay me now? . . .

EDMOND: Yes. Certainly.

(He takes out his wallet, hands her a credit card.)

WHORE: I need cash, honey.

EDMOND: They said at the door I could pay with my . . .

WHORE: . . . That was at the door . . . you have to pay *me* with *cash*. . . .

EDMOND: I don't think I *have* it. . . . *(He checks through his wallet.)* I don't *have* it. . . .

WHORE: How much do you have? . . .

EDMOND: I, uh, only have *sixty*.

WHORE: Jeez, I'm *sorry*, honey, but I can't *do* it. . . .

EDMOND: Well, wait, wait, wait, wait, maybe we could . . . wait. . . .

WHORE: Why don't you *get* it, and come *back* here. . . .

EDMOND: Well, where could I *get* it? . . .

WHORE: Go to a restaurant and cash a check, I'll be here till *four*. . . .

EDMOND: I'll. I'll . . . um, um . . . *yes. Thank you.* . . .

WHORE: Not at all.

(**EDMOND** *leaves the whorehouse.*)

Scene Ten.
Three-Card Monte.

EDMOND *out on the street, passes by the three-card-monte men, who have assembled again.*

SHARPER: You can't win if you don't play. . . . *(To* EDMOND) *You,* sir . . .

EDMOND: Me? . . .

SHARPER: You going to try me again? . . .

EDMOND: Again? . . .

SHARPER: *I* remember you beat me out of that *fifty* that time with your girlfriend. . . .

EDMOND: . . . When was this?

SHARPER: On four*teen*ff street. . . . You going to try me one more time? . . .

EDMOND: Uh . . . .

SHARPER: . . . Play you for that fifty. . . . Fifty get you one hundred, we see you as fast as you was. . . .
Pay on the red, pass on the black. . . .
Where is the queen? . . . You pick the queen you win. . . .
Where is the queen? . . . Who saw the queen? . . .
You put up fifty, win a hundred. . . . Now: Who saw the queen? . . .

SHILL: I got her!

SHARPER: How much? Put your money up. How much?

SHILL: I bet you fifty dollars.

SHARPER: Put it up.

*(The **SHILL** does so. The **SHILL** turns a card.)*

SHILL: There!

SHARPER: My man, I'm jus' too quick for you today.
Who saw the queen? We got two cards left.
Pay on the *red* queen, who saw her?

EDMOND: I saw her.

SHARPER: Ah, *shit*, man, you too fass for me.

EDMOND: . . . For fifty dollars . . .

SHARPER: All right—all right.
Put it up. *(Pause.)*

EDMOND: Will you pay me if I win?

SHARPER: Yes, I will. If you win. But you got to *win* first. . . .

EDMOND: All that I've got to do is turn the queen.

SHARPER: Thass all you got to do.

EDMOND: I'll bet you fifty.

SHARPER: You sure?

EDMOND: Yes. I'm sure.

SHARPER: Put it up. (**EDMOND** *does so.*) Now: Which one you like?

EDMOND *(turning card):* There!

SHARPER *(taking money):* I'm *sorry,* my man. This time you lose—
now we even. Take another shot. You pick the queen you win . . . bet you another fifty. . . .

EDMOND: Let me see those cards.

SHARPER: These cards are fine, it's you thass slow.

EDMOND: I want to see the cards.

SHARPER: These cards are good my man, you *lost.*

EDMOND: You let me see those cards.

SHARPER: You ain't goin' *see* no motherfuckin' cards, man, we playin' a *game* here. . . .

SHILL: . . . You lost, *get* lost.

EDMOND: Give me those cards, fella.

SHARPER: You want to see the cards? You want to see the cards? . . . *Here* is the motherfuckin' cards. . . .

*(He hits **EDMOND** in the face. He and the **SHILL** beat **EDMOND** for several seconds. **EDMOND** falls to the ground.)*

Scene Eleven.
A Hotel.

EDMOND, *torn and battered, comes up to the* DESK CLERK.

EDMOND: I want a room.

CLERK: Twenty-two dollars. *(Pause.)*

EDMOND: I lost my wallet.

CLERK: Go to the police.

EDMOND: You can call up American Express.

CLERK: Go to the police. *(Pause.)*
I don't want to hear it.

EDMOND: You can call the credit-card people. I have insurance.

CLERK: Call them yourself. Right across the hall.

EDMOND: I have no money.

CLERK: I'm sure it's a free call.

EDMOND: Do those phones require a dime?

CLERK *(Pause):*   I'm sure I don't know.

EDMOND: You know if they need a *dime* or not.
To get a *dial* tone . . . You know if they need a *dime,*
for chrissake. Do you want to live in this kind of world?
Do you want to live in a *world* like that? I've been *hurt?*
Are you *blind?* Would you appreciate it if I acted this
way to *you? (Pause.)*
I *asked* you one simple thing.
Do they need a *dime?*

CLERK: No. They don't need a dime. Now, you make
your call, and you go somewhere else.

Scene Twelve.
The Pawnshop.

The **OWNER** *waiting on a customer who is perusing objects in the display counter.*

CUSTOMER: Whaddaya get for that? What is that? Fourteen or eighteen karat?

OWNER: Fourteen.

CUSTOMER: Yeah? Lemme see that. How much is that?

OWNER: Six hundred eighty-five.

CUSTOMER: Why is that? How old is that? Is that *old?*

OWNER: You know how much *gold* that you got in there?
Feel. That. Just feel that.

CUSTOMER: Where is it marked?

OWNER: Right there. You want that loupe?

CUSTOMER: No. I can see it.

(**EDMOND** *comes into the store and stands by the two.*)

OWNER *(to* **EDMOND***)*: What?

EDMOND: I want to pawn something.

OWNER: Talk to the man in back.

CUSTOMER: What else you got like this?

OWNER: I don't know *what* I got. You're *looking* at it.

CUSTOMER *(pointing to item in display case)*: Lemme see that.

EDMOND *(goes to* **MAN IN BACK** *behind grate)*: I want to pawn something.

MAN: What?

EDMOND: My ring.

(Holds up hand.)

MAN: Take it off.

EDMOND: It's difficult to take it off.

MAN: Spit on it.

(**EDMOND** *does so.)*

CUSTOMER: How much is that?

OWNER: Two hundred twenty.

EDMOND *(happily):* I got it off.

(**EDMOND** *hands the ring to the* **MAN.**)

MAN: What do you want to do with this?
You want to pawn it.

EDMOND: Yes. How does that work?

MAN: Is that what you want to do?

EDMOND: Yes. Are there other things to do?

MAN: . . . What you can *do,* no, I mean, if you
wanted it *appraised* . . .

EDMOND: . . . Uh-huh . . .

MAN: . . . or want to *sell* it . . .

EDMOND: . . . Uh-huh . . .

MAN: . . . or you wanted it to *pawn.* . . .

EDMOND: I understand.

MAN: Alright?

EDMOND: How much is getting it appraised?

MAN: Five dollars.

CUSTOMER: Lemme see something in black.

EDMOND: What would you give me if I pawned it?

MAN: What do you want for it?

EDMOND: What is it worth?

MAN: You pawn it all you're gonna get's approximately . . . You know how this works?

CUSTOMER: Yes. Let me see that. . . .

EDMOND: No.

MAN: What you get, a quarter of the value.

EDMOND: Mm.

MAN: Approximately. For a year. You're paying twelve percent. You can redeem your pledge with the year you pay your twelve percent. To that time. Plus the amount of the loan.

EDMOND: What is my pledge?

MAN: Well, that depends on what it *is*.

EDMOND: What do you mean?

MAN: What it *is*. Do you understand?

EDMOND: No.

MAN: Whatever the amount *is*, that is your pledge.

EDMOND: The amount of the loan.

MAN: That's right.

EDMOND: I understand.

MAN: Alright. What are you looking for, the ring?

CUSTOMER: Nope. Not today. I'll catch you next time. Lemme see that knife.

EDMOND: What is it worth?

MAN: The most I can give you, hundred and twenty bucks.

CUSTOMER: This is nice.

EDMOND: I'll take it.

MAN: Good. I'll be right back. Give me the ring.

(EDMOND *does so.* EDMOND *wanders over to watch the other transaction.*)

CUSTOMER *(holding up knife):* What are you asking for this?

OWNER: Twenty-three bucks. Say, twenty bucks.

CUSTOMER *(to himself):* Twenty bucks . . .

EDMOND: Why is it so expensive?

OWNER: Why is it so expensive?

CUSTOMER: No. I'm going to pass. *(He hands knife back, exiting.)* I'll catch you later.

OWNER: Right.

EDMOND: Why is the knife so expensive?

OWNER: This is a *survival* knife. G.I. Issue. World War Two. And that is why.

EDMOND: Survival knife.

OWNER: That is correct.

EDMOND: Is it a good knife?

OWNER: It is the best knife that money can buy.

(He starts to put knife away. As an afterthought) You want it?

EDMOND: Let me think about it for a moment.

Scene Thirteen.
The Subway.

EDMOND *is in the subway. Waiting with him is a* WOMAN *in a hat.*

EDMOND *(Pause):* My mother had a hat like that. *(Pause.)* My mother had a hat like that. *(Pause.)* I . . . I'm not making conversation. She wore it for years. She had it when I was a child.

(The WOMAN *starts to walk away.* EDMOND *grabs her)*

I wasn't just making it "up." It *happened.* . . .

WOMAN *(detaching herself from his grip):* Excuse me. . . .

EDMOND: . . . who the fuck do you think you *are?* . . .
I'm *talking* to you . . . What am I? A *stone?* . . .
Did I say, "I want to lick your pussy? . . ."
I said, "My mother had that same hat. . . ."
You *cunt* . . . What am I? A *dog?* I'd like to slash your

fucking *face* . . . I'd like to slash your motherfucking *face* apart. . . .

WOMAN: . . . WILL SOMEBODY *HELP* ME. . . .

EDMOND: *You* don't know who I am. . . . *(She breaks free.)*
Is everybody in this town *insane?* . . . Fuck you . . . fuck you . . . fuck you . . . fuck the *lot* of you . . . fuck you *all* . . . I don't *need* you . . . I worked all of my life!

Scene Fourteen.

On the Street, Outside the Peep Show.

PIMP: What are you looking for?

EDMOND: What?

PIMP: What are you looking for?

EDMOND: I'm not looking for a goddamn thing.

PIMP: You looking for that *joint*, it's *closed*.

EDMOND: What joint?

PIMP: That *joint* that you was looking for.

EDMOND: Thank you, no. I'm not looking for that joint.

PIMP: You looking for *something*, and I think that I know what you looking for.

EDMOND: You do?

PIMP: You come with me, I get you what you want.

EDMOND: What do I want?

PIMP: *I* know. We get you some *action,* my friend. We get you something sweet to shoot on. *(Pause.)* I know. Thass what I'm doing here.

EDMOND: What are you saying?

PIMP: I'm saying that we going to find you something nice.

EDMOND: You're saying that you're going to find me a woman.

PIMP: Thass what I'm *doing* out here, friend.

EDMOND: How much?

PIMP: Well, how much do you want?

EDMOND: I want somebody clean.

PIMP: Thass right.

EDMOND: I want a blow-job.

PIMP: Alright.

EDMOND: How much?

PIMP: Thirty bucks.

EDMOND: That's too much.

PIMP: How much do you want to *spen'?* . . .

EDMOND: Say fifteen dollars.

PIMP: Twenny-five.

EDMOND: No. Twenty.

PIMP: Yes.

EDMOND: Is that alright?

PIMP: Give me the twenty.

EDMOND: I'll give it to you when we see the girl.

PIMP: Hey, I'm not going to *leave* you, man, you *coming* with me. We *goin'* to see the girl.

EDMOND: Good, I'll give it to you then.

PIMP: You give it to me *now*, you unnerstan'? Huh? *(Pause.)* Thass the trans*action. (Pause.)* You see? Unless you were a *cop. (Pause.)* You give me the *money*, and then thass en*trap*ment. *(Pause.)* You understand?

EDMOND: Yes. I'm not a cop.

PIMP: Alright.

Do you *see* what I'm saying?

EDMOND: I'm sorry.

PIMP: Thass alright. (**EDMOND** *takes out wallet. Exchange of money.)* You come with me. Now we'll just walk here like we're talking.

EDMOND: Is she going to be clean?

PIMP: Yes, she is. I understand you, man.

(Pause. They walk.)

I understand what you want. *(Pause.)* Believe me. *(Pause.)*

EDMOND: Is there any money in this?

PIMP: Well, you know, man, there's *some* . . . you get done piecing off the *police*, this man *here* . . . the *medical*, the *bills, you* know.

EDMOND: How much does the girl get?

PIMP: Sixty percent.

EDMOND: Mm.

PIMP: *Oh* yeah. *(He indicates a spot.)* Up here.

*(They walk to the spot. The **PIMP** takes out a knife and holds it to **EDMOND**'s neck.)*

Now give me all you' money mothafucka! *Now!*

EDMOND: Alright.

PIMP: *All* of it. Don't turn aroun' . . . don't turn aroun' . . . just put it in my hand.

EDMOND: Alright.

PIMP: . . . And don't you make a motherfuckin' sound. . . .

EDMOND: I'm going to do everything that you say. . . .

PIMP: Now you just han' me all you got.

(**EDMOND** *turns, strikes the* **PIMP** *in the face.*)

EDMOND: YOU MOTHERFUCKING NIGGER!

PIMP: Hold on. . . .

EDMOND: You motherfucking *shit* . . . you *jungle* bunny . . . *(He strikes the* **PIMP** *again. He drops his knife.)*

PIMP: I . . .

EDMOND: You *coon,* you *cunt,* you *cock*sucker . . .

PIMP: I . . .

EDMOND: "Take me upstairs? . . ."

PIMP: Oh, my God . . . *(The* **PIMP** *has fallen to the sidewalk and* **EDMOND** *is kicking him.)*

EDMOND: You *fuck.* You *nigger.* You dumb *cunt* . . . You *shit* . . . You shit . . . *(Pause.)* You fucking *nigger. (Pause.)* Don't fuck with *me,* you *coon.* . . .

(Pause. **EDMOND** *spits on him.)*

I hope you're *dead.*

(Pause.)

Don't fuck with *me,* you *coon.* . . .

(Pause. **EDMOND** *spits on him.)*

Scene Fifteen.

The Coffeehouse.

EDMOND *seated in the coffeehouse, addresses the waitress,* **GLENNA.**

EDMOND: I want a cup of coffee. No. A beer. Beer chaser. Irish whiskey.

GLENNA: Irish whiskey.

EDMOND: Yes. A double. Huh.

GLENNA: You're in a peppy mood today.

EDMOND: You're goddamn right I am, and you want me to tell you *why?* Because I am *alive.* You know how much of our life we're alive, you and me? *Nothing.* Two minutes out of the year. You know, you know, we're *sheltered.* . . .

GLENNA: Who is?

EDMOND: You and I. White people. All of us. All of us. We're doomed. The white race is doomed. And do you know *why?* . . . Sit down. . . .

GLENNA: I can't. I'm working.

EDMOND: And do you know *why*—you can do anything you *want* to do, you don't sit down because you're *"working,"* the reason you don't sit down is you don't *want* to sit down, because it's more comfortable to *accept* a law than question it and live your life. All of us. *All* of us. We've bred the life out of ourselves. And we live in a fog. We live in a dream. Our life is a *school*-house, and we're dead.

(Pause.)

How old are you?

GLENNA: Twenty-eight.

EDMOND: I've lived in a fog for thirty-four years. Most of the life I have to live. It's gone.
It's gone. I wasted it. Because I didn't know. And you know what the answer is? To *live. (Pause.)*
I want to go home with you tonight.

GLENNA: Why?

EDMOND: Why do you think? I want to fuck you. *(Pause.)* It's as simple as that.
What's your name?

GLENNA: Glenna. *(Pause.)* What's yours?

EDMOND: Edmond.

Scene Sixteen
Glenna's Apartment.

EDMOND *and* **GLENNA** *are lounging around semiclothed.* **EDMOND** *shows* **GLENNA** *the survival knife.*

EDMOND: You see this?

GLENNA: Yes.

EDMOND: That fucking nigger comes up to me, what am I fitted to do. He comes up, "Give me all your money." Thirty-four years fits me to sweat and say he's underpaid, and he can't get a *job*, he's *bigger* than me . . . he's a *killer*, he don't care about his *life*, you understand, so he'd do *anything*. . . .
Eh? That's what I'm fitted to do. In a mess of intellectuality to wet my *pants* while this *coon* cuts my *dick* off . . . eh? Because I'm taught to *hate*.
I want to tell you something. Something *spoke* to me, I got a *shock* (I don't know, I got mad . . .), I got a *shock*, and I spoke *back* to him. "Up your *ass*, you *coon* . . . you want to fight, *I'll* fight you, I'll cut out your fuckin' *heart*, eh, *I* don't give a fuck. . . ."

GLENNA: Yes.

EDMOND: Eh? I'm saying, "*I* don't give a fuck, *I* got some warlike blood in *my* veins, too, you fucking *spade*, you coon. . . ." The *blood* ran down his neck. . . .

GLENNA *(looking at knife):* With *that?*

EDMOND: You bet your ass. . . .

GLENNA: Did you kill him?

EDMOND: Did I kill him?

GLENNA: Yes.

EDMOND: I don't care. *(Pause.)*

GLENNA: That's wonderful.

EDMOND: And in that *moment* . . .
when I *spoke,* you understand, 'cause that was more important than the *knife,* when I spoke *back* to him, I DIDN'T FUCKING WANT TO *UNDERSTAND* . . . let *him* understand *me* . . .
I wanted to KILL him. *(Pause.)* In that *moment* thirty years of prejudice came out of me. *(Pause.)* Thirty *years.* Of all those um um um of all those *cleaning* ladies . . .

GLENNA: . . . Uh-huh . . .

EDMOND: . . . uh? . . . who *might* have broke the lamp. SO WHAT? You understand? For the first *time,* I swear to god, for the first *time* I saw: THEY'RE PEO-PLE, TOO.

GLENNA *(pause):* Do you know who I hate?

EDMOND: Who is that?

GLENNA: ~~Faggots~~. gay men

EDMOND: Yes. I hate them, too. And you know *why?*

GLENNA: Why?

EDMOND: They suck cock. *(Pause.)* And that's the truest thing you'll ever hear.

GLENNA: I hate them 'cause they don't like women.

EDMOND: They *hate* women.

GLENNA: I know that they do.

EDMOND: It makes you feel good to *say* it? Doesn't it?

GLENNA: Yes.

EDMOND: Then *say* it. *Say* it. If it makes you whole. *Always* say it. *Always* for your*self* . . .

GLENNA: It's hard.

EDMOND: *Yes.*

GLENNA: Sometimes it's hard.

EDMOND: You're goddamn right it's hard. And there's a *reason* why it's hard.

GLENNA: Why?

EDMOND: So that we will stand up. So that we'll be our*selves.* Glenna: *(Pause.)* Glenna: This world is a piece of shit. *(Pause.)* It is a shit house. *(Pause.)* . . . There is NO *LAW* . . . there is no *history* . . . there is just *now* . . . and if there is a *god* he may love the weak, Glenna. *(Pause.)* but he respects the strong. *(Pause.)* And if you are a *man* you should be feared. *(Pause.)* You should be *feared.* . . . *(Pause.)* You just know you command respect.

GLENNA: That's why I love the Theater. . . . *(Pause.)* Because what you must ask respect for is yourself. . . .

EDMOND: What do you mean?

GLENNA: When you're on stage.

EDMOND: Yes.

GLENNA: For *your* feelings.

EDMOND: Absolutely. Absolutely, yes . . .

GLENNA: And, and, and *not* be someone else.

EDMOND: Why should you? . . .

GLENNA: . . . That's why, and I'm so proud to *be* in this profession . . .

EDMOND: . . . I don't blame you . . .

GLENNA: . . . because your aspirations . . .

EDMOND: . . . and I'll bet that you're good at it. . . .

GLENNA: . . . they . . .

EDMOND: . . . They have no bounds.

GLENNA: There's nothing . . .

EDMOND: . . . Yes. I understand. . . .

GLENNA: . . . to *bound* you but your soul.

EDMOND *(pause):* Do something for me.

GLENNA: . . . Uh . . .

EDMOND: *Act* something for me. Would you act something for me? . . .

GLENNA: *Now?*

EDMOND: Yes.

GLENNA: Sitting right here? . . .

EDMOND: Yes. *(Pause.)*

GLENNA: Would you really like me to?

EDMOND: You know I would. You see me sitting here, and you know that I would. I'd *love* it. Just because we both *want* to. I'd *love* you to. *(Pause.)*

GLENNA: What would you like me to do?

EDMOND: Whatever you'd like. What plays have you done?

GLENNA: Well, we've only done scenes.

EDMOND: You've only done scenes.

GLENNA: I shouldn't say "only." They contain the kernel of the play.

EDMOND: Uh-huh.

(Pause.)

What *plays* have you done?

GLENNA: In college I played Juliet.

EDMOND: In Shakespeare?

GLENNA: Yes. In Shakespeare. What do you think?

EDMOND: Well, I meant, there's *plays* named Juliet.

GLENNA: There are?

EDMOND: Yes.

GLENNA: I don't think so.

EDMOND: Well, there are. —Don't. Don't. Don't. Don't be so *limited*. . . . And don't assume I'm dumb because I wear a suit and tie.

GLENNA: I don't assume that.

EDMOND: Because what we've *done* tonight. Since you met me, it didn't make a difference then. Forget it. All I meant, you say you are an *actress*. . . .

GLENNA: I am an actress. . . .

EDMOND: Yes. I say that's what you *say*. So *I* say what *plays* have you done. That's all.

GLENNA: The work I've done I have done for my peers.

EDMOND: What does that mean?

GLENNA: In class.

EDMOND: In class.

GLENNA: In class or workshop.

EDMOND: Not, not for a paying group.

GLENNA: No, absolutely not.

EDMOND: Then you are not an actress. Face it.
Let's start right. The two of us. I'm not lying to *you*, don't lie to *me*.
And don't lie to yourself.
Face it. You're a beautiful woman. You have *worlds* before you. I do, too.
Things to do. Things you can di*scover*.
What I'm saying, start *now*, start *tonight*. With *me*. *Be* with me. Be what you *are*. . . .

GLENNA: I am what I am.

EDMOND: That's absolutely right. And that's what I loved when I saw you tonight. What I *loved*.
I use that word. *(Pause.)* I used that word.
I loved a *woman*. Standing there. A working woman. Who brought life to what she did. Who took a moment to *joke* with me. That's . . . that's . . . that's . . . god *bless* you what you are. Say it: I am a waitress.

(Pause.)

Say it.

GLENNA: What does it mean if I say something?

EDMOND: Say it with me. *(Pause.)*

GLENNA: What?

EDMOND: "I am a waitress."

GLENNA: I think that you better go.

EDMOND: If you want me to go I'll go. Say it with me. Say what you are. And I'll say what *I* am.

GLENNA: . . . What *you* are . . .

EDMOND: I've *made* that discovery. Now: I want you to change your life with me. *Right* now, for what-*ever* that we can be. *I* don't know what that is, *you* don't know. Speak with me. Right now. Say it.

GLENNA: I don't know what you're talking about.

EDMOND: Oh, by the Lord, yes, you do. Say it with me. *(She takes out a vial of pills.)* What are those?

GLENNA: Pills.

EDMOND: For what? Don't take them.

GLENNA: I have this tendency to get anxious.

EDMOND *(knocks them from her hand):* Don't take them. Go *ihrough* it. Go *through* with me.

GLENNA: You're scaring me.

EDMOND: I am not. I know when I'm scaring you. *Believe me. (Pause.)*

GLENNA: Get out. *(Pause.)*

EDMOND: Glenna. *(Pause.)*

GLENNA: Get out! GET OUT GET OUT! LEAVE ME THE FUCK ALONE!!! WHAT DID I DO, PLEDGE MY LIFE TO YOU? I LET YOU FUCK ME. GO AWAY.

EDMOND: Listen to me: You know what madness is?

GLENNA: I told you go away. *(Goes to phone. Dials.)*

EDMOND: I'm lonely, too. I know what it is, too. Believe me. Do you know what madness is?

GLENNA *(into phone):* Susie? . . .

EDMOND: It's self-indulgence.

GLENNA: Suse, can you come over here? . . .

EDMOND: Will you please put that *down?* You know how *rare* this is? . . .

(He knocks the phone out of her hands. **GLENNA** *cowers.)*

GLENNA: Oh fuck . . .

EDMOND: Don't be ridiculous. I'm *talking* to you.

GLENNA: Don't hurt me. No. No. I can't deal with this.

EDMOND: Don't be ridic . . .

GLENNA: I . . . No. Help! Help.

EDMOND: . . . You're being . . .

GLENNA: . . . HELP!

EDMOND: . . . are you *insane?* What the fuck are you trying to *do,* for godsake?

GLENNA: HELP!

EDMOND: You want to wake the *neighbors?*

GLENNA: WILL SOMEBODY HELP ME? . . .

EDMOND: Shut up shut up!

GLENNA: Will somebody help you are the get *away* from me! You are the *devil.* I know who you are. I know what you want me to do. Get *away* from me I curse *you,* you can't kill me, get away from me I'm *good.*

EDMOND: *WILL YOU SHUT THE FUCK UP?* You fucking *bitch.*
You're *nuts.* . . .
(He stabs her with the knife.)

Are you *insane?* Are you *insane,* you fucking *idiot?* . . .
You stupid fucking *bitch* . . .
You stupid fucking . . . *now* look what you've done.
(Pause.)
Now look what you've blood fucking done.

Scene Seventeen
The Mission.

EDMOND *is attracted by the speech of a* **MISSION PREACHER**. *He walks to the front of the mission and listens outside the mission doors.*

PREACHER: "Oh no, not me!" You say, "Oh no, not me. Not *me*, Lord, to whom you hold out your hand. Not *me* to whom you offer your eternal grace. Not *me* who can be saved. . . ."
But *who* but you, I ask you? *Who* but you.
You say you are a grievous sinner? He *knows* that you are. You say he does not know the *depth* of my iniquity. *Believe* me, friends, he does. And still you say, he does not know—you say this in your secret soul—he does not know the terrible depth of my unbelief.
Believe me friends, he knows that too.
To *all* of you who say his grace is not meant to extend to one as black as you I say to WHO but you? To you *alone*. Not to the blessed. You think that Christ died for the blessed? That he died for the heavenly hosts? That did not make him God, my friends, it does not need a God to sacrifice for angels. It required a God to sacrifice for MAN. You hear me? For *you* . . . there is *none* so black but that he died for you. He died *especially* for you.

Upon my life. On the graves of my family, and by the surety I have of his Eternal Bliss HE DIED FOR YOU AND YOU ARE SAVED. Praise *God,* my friends. Praise God and testify. Who will come up and testify with me, my friends? *(Pause.)*

WOMAN *from subway walks by. She sees* **EDMOND** *and stares at him.*

EDMOND *(speaks up):*   I will testify.

PREACHER: *Who* is that?

EDMOND: I will testify.

PREACHER: Sweet *God,* let that man come up here!

(EDMOND *starts into the church.)*

WOMAN *(shouts):*   That's the man! Someone! Call a policeman! That's the man!

PREACHER: . . . Who will come open up his soul? Alleluia, my friends. *Be* with me.

WOMAN: That's the man. *Stop* him!
(EDMOND *stops and turns. He looked wonderingly at the* **WOMAN,** *then starts inside.)*

POLICEMAN: Just a moment, sir.

EDMOND: I . . . I . . . I . . . I . . . I'm on my way to church.

PREACHER: Sweet *Jesus,* let that man come forth. . . .

WOMAN: That's the man tried to rape me on the train. He had a knife. . . .

EDMOND: . . . There must be some mistake. . . .

WOMAN: He tried to rape me on the train.

EDMOND: . . . There's some mistake, I'm on my way to church. . . .

POLICEMAN: What's the trouble here?

EDMOND: No trouble, I'm on my way into the mission.

WOMAN: This man tried to rape me on the train yesterday.

EDMOND: Obviously this woman's mad.

PREACHER: Will no one come forth?

EDMOND: I . . . I . . . I . . . have to go into the church.

POLICEMAN: Could I see some identification please?

EDMOND: Please, officer, I haven't time. I . . . I . . . it's been a long . . . I don't have my *wallet* on me. My name's Gregory Brock. I live at 428 Twenty-second Street, I own the building. I . . . I have to go inside the church.

POLICEMAN: You want to show me some ID?

EDMOND: I don't have any. I told you.

POLICEMAN: You're going to have to come with me.

EDMOND: I . . . please . . . Yes. In one minute. Not . . . not now, I have to *preach.* . . .

POLICEMAN: Come on.

EDMOND: You're, you're, you're making a . . .

EDMOND: Please. Let me go. And I'll come with you afterward.
I swear that I will. I swear it on my life.
There's been a mistake. I'm an elder in this church.
Come *with* me if you will.
I have to go and speak.

POLICEMAN: Look. *(Conciliatorily, he puts an arm on* **EDMOND.** *He feels something. He pulls back.)* What's that?

EDMOND: It's nothing. *(The* **POLICEMAN** *pulls out the survival knife.)* It's a knife. It's there for self-protection.

(The **POLICEMAN** *throws* **EDMOND** *to the ground and handcuffs him.)*

Scene Eighteen.
The Interrogation.

EDMOND *and an* INTERROGATOR *at the police station.*

INTERROGATOR: What was the knife for?

EDMOND: For protection.

INTERROGATOR: From whom?

EDMOND: Everyone.

INTERROGATOR: You know that it's illegal?

EDMOND: No.

INTERROGATOR: It is.

EDMOND *(pause):* I'm sorry.

INTERROGATOR: Speaking to that woman in the way you did is construed as assault.

EDMOND: I never spoke to her.

INTERROGATOR: She identified you as the man who accosted her last evening on the subway.

EDMOND: She is seriously mistaken.

INTERROGATOR: If she presses charges you'll be arraigned for assault.

EDMOND: For *speaking* to her?

INTERROGATOR: You admit that you were speaking to her?

EDMOND *(pause):* I want to ask you something. *(Pause.)*

INTERROGATOR: Alright.

EDMOND: Did you ever kick a dog?

(Pause.)

Well, that's what I did. Man to man. That's what I did. I made a simple, harmless comment to her, she responded like a fucking bitch.

INTERROGATOR: You trying to pick her up?

EDMOND: Why should I try to pick her up?

INTERROGATOR: She was an attractive woman.

EDMOND: She was *not* an attractive woman.

INTERROGATOR: You gay?

EDMOND: What business is that of yours?

INTERROGATOR: Are you?

EDMOND: No.

INTERROGATOR: You married?

EDMOND: Yes. In fact, I was going back to my wife.

INTERROGATOR: You were going back to your wife?

EDMOND: I was going home to her.

INTERROGATOR: You said you were going back to her, what did you mean?

EDMOND: I'd left my wife, alright?

INTERROGATOR: You left your wife.

EDMOND: Yes.

INTERROGATOR: Why?

EDMOND: I was *bored.* Didn't that ever happen to *you?*

INTERROGATOR: And why did you lie to the officer?

EDMOND: What officer?

INTERROGATOR: Who picked you up. There's no Gregory Brock at the address you gave. You didn't give him your right name.

EDMOND: I was embarrassed.

INTERROGATOR: Why?

EDMOND: I didn't have my wallet.

INTERROGATOR: Why?

EDMOND: I'd left it at home.

INTERROGATOR: And why did that embarrass you?

EDMOND: I don't know. I have had no *sleep.* I just want to go *home.* I am a *solid . . .* look: My name is Edmond Burke, I live at 485 West Seventy-ninth Street. I work at Stearns and Harrington. I had a tiff with my wife. I went out on the town. I've learned my lesson. *Believe* me. I just want to go home. Whatever I've done I'll make right. *(Pause.)* Alright? *(Pause.)* Alright? These things happen and then they're done. When he *stopped* me I was going to church. I've been unwell. I'll confess to you that I've been confused, but, but . . . I've learned my lesson and I'm ready to go home.

INTERROGATOR: Why did you kill that girl?

EDMOND: What girl?

INTERROGATOR: That girl you killed.

Scene Nineteen.
Jail.

EDMOND*'s* WIFE *is visiting him. They sit across from each other in silence for a while.*

EDMOND: How's everything?

WIFE: Fine. *(Pause.)*

EDMOND: I'm alright, too.

WIFE: Good. *(Pause.)*

EDMOND: You want to tell me you're *mad* at me or something?

WIFE: Did you kill that girl in her apartment?

EDMOND: Yes, but I want to tell you something. . . . I didn't mean to. But do you want to hear something *funny?* . . . (Now, don't laugh. . . .) I think I'd just had too much coffee. *(Pause.)*
I'll tell you something else: I think there are just too many people in the world. I think that's why we kill each other *(Pause.)* I . . . I . . . I suppose you're mad

at me for leaving you. *(Pause.)* I don't suppose you're, uh, inclined (or, nor do I think you should be) to stand by me. I understand that. *(Pause.)* I'm sure that there are marriages where the wife would. Or the husband if it would go that way. *(Pause.)* But I know ours is not one of that type.

(Pause.) I know that you *wished* at one point it would be. I wished that too.

At one point. *(Pause.)*

I know at certain times we wished we could be . . . closer to each other. I can say that now. I'm sure this is the way you feel when someone near you dies. You never said the things you wanted desperately to say. It would have been so simple to say them. *(Pause.)* But you never did.

WIFE: You got the papers?

EDMOND: Yes.

WIFE: Good.

EDMOND: Oh, yes. I got them.

WIFE: Anything you need?

EDMOND: No. Can't think of a thing.

(The WIFE *stands up, starts gathering her things together.)*

You take care, now!

Scene Twenty.
The New Cell.

EDMOND *is put in his new cell. His cellmate is a large, black* PRISONER. EDMOND *sits on his new bunk in silence awhile.*

EDMOND: You know, you know, you know, you know we can't distinguish between *anxiety* and *fear*. Do you know what I mean? I don't mean fear. I mean, I *do* mean "fear," I, I don't mean *anxiety*. (Pause.) We . . . when we *fear* things I think that we *wish* for them. (Pause.) Death. Or "burglars." (Pause.) Don't you think? We mean we *wish* they would come. Every fear hides a wish. Don't you think?

(A pause.)

I always knew that I would end up here. (Pause.) (To himself) Every fear hides a wish. I think I'm going to like it here.

PRISONER: You do?

EDMOND: Yes, I do. Do you know why? It's simple. That's why I think that I am. You know, I always thought that *white* people should be in prison. I know it's the black race we keep there. But I thought *we* should be there. You know why?

PRISONER: Why?

EDMOND: To be with black people. *(Pause.)* Does that sound too *simple* to you? *(Pause.)*

PRISONER: No.

EDMOND: Because we're *lonely. (Pause.)*
But what I *know* . . . *(Pause.)* What I *know* I think that all this *fear*, this fucking *fear* we feel must hide a wish. 'Cause I don't feel it since I'm here. I *don't*. I think the first time in my life. *(Pause.)* In my whole adult life I don't feel fearful since I came in here.
I think we are like birds. I think that humans are like birds. We suspect when there's going to be an *earthquake*. Birds know. They leave three days earlier. Something in their soul responds.

PRISONER: The birds leave when there's going to be an earthquake?

EDMOND: Yes. And I think, in our soul, *we, we* feel, we sense there is going to be . . .

PRISONER: . . . Uh-huh . . .

EDMOND: . . . a cataclysm. But we cannot flee. We're fearful. All the time. Because we can't trust what we know. That ringing. *(Pause.)*
I think we feel. Something tells us, "Get *out* of here." *(Pause.)*
White people feel that. Do you feel that? *(Pause.)* Well. But I don't feel it since I'm here. *(Pause.)* I don't feel it

since I'm here. I think I've settled. So, so, so I must be somewhere safe. Isn't that funny?

PRISONER: No.

EDMOND: You think it's not?

PRISONER: Yes.

EDMOND: Thank you.

PRISONER: Thass alright.

EDMOND: Huh. *(Pause.)*

PRISONER: You want a cigarette?

EDMOND: No, thank you. Not just now.

PRISONER: Thass alright.

EDMOND: Maybe later.

PRISONER: Sure. Now you know what?

EDMOND: What?

PRISONER: I think you should just get on my body.

EDMOND: I, yes. What do you mean?

PRISONER: You should get on my body now.

EDMOND: I don't know what that means.

PRISONER: It means to suck my dick. *(Pause.)* Now don't you want to do that?

EDMOND: No.

PRISONER: Well, you jes' do it anyway.

EDMOND: You're joking.

PRISONER: Not at all.

EDMOND: I don't think I could do that.

PRISONER: Well, you going to try or you going to die. Les' get this out the way. *(Pause.)* I'm not no going to repeat myself.

EDMOND: I'll scream.

PRISONER: You *scream,* and you offend me. You are going to die. Look at me now and say I'm foolin'. *(Pause.)*

EDMOND: I . . . I . . . I . . . I . . . I can't, I can't do, I . . . I . . .

PRISONER: The mother*fuck* you can't. *Right* now, missy.

(The **PRISONER** *slaps* **EDMOND** *viciously several times.)*

Right now, Jim. An' you bes' be nice.

Scene Twenty-one.
The Chaplain.

EDMOND *is sitting across from the* PRISON CHAPLAIN.

CHAPLAIN: You don't have to talk.

EDMOND: I don't want to talk. *(Pause.)*

CHAPLAIN: Are you getting accustomed to life here?

EDMOND: Do you know what happened to me?

CHAPLAIN: No. *(Pause.)*

EDMOND: I was sodomized.

CHAPLAIN: Did you report it?

EDMOND: Yes.

CHAPLAIN: What did they say?

EDMOND: "That happens." *(Pause.)*

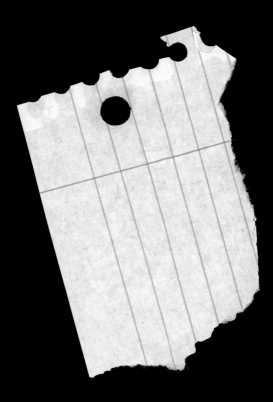

CHAPLAIN: I'm sorry it happened to you. *(Pause.)*

EDMOND: Thank you.

CHAPLAIN *(pause):* Are you lonely?

EDMOND: Yes. *(Pause.)* Yes. *(Pause.)* I feel so *alone.* . . .

CHAPLAIN: Shhhhh . . .

EDMOND: I'm so *empty.* . . .

CHAPLAIN: Maybe you are ready to be *filled.*

EDMOND: That's *bullshit,* that's *bullshit.* That's pious *bullshit.*

CHAPLAIN: Is it?

EDMOND: Yes.

CHAPLAIN: That you are ready to be filled? Is it impossible?

EDMOND: Yes. Yes. I don't know what's impossible.

CHAPLAIN: Nothing is impossible.

EDMOND: Oh. Nothing is impossible. Not to "God," is that what you're saying?

CHAPLAIN: Yes.

EDMOND: Well, then, you're full of *shit.* You understand that. If nothing's impossible to God, then let him let me walk *out* of here and be *free.* Let him cause a new *day.* In a perfect land full of *life.* And *air.* Where

people are *kind* to each other, and there's *work* to do. Where we grow up in *love*, and in security we're *wanted. (Pause.)*
Let him do that.
Let him.
Tell him to do that. *(Pause.)* You *ass*hole—if nothing's impossible . . . I think *that* must be *easy.* . . . Not: "Let me *fly*," or, "If there is a God make him to make the *sun* come out at night." Go on. Please. Please. Please. I'm *begging* you. If you're so smart. Let him do that: Let him do that. *(Pause.)* Please. *(Pause.)* Please. I'm begging you.

CHAPLAIN: Are you sorry that you killed that girl?

(Pause.)

Edmond?

EDMOND: Yes. *(Pause.)*

CHAPLAIN: Are you sorry that you killed that girl?

EDMOND: I'm sorry about everything.

CHAPLAIN: But are you sorry that you killed? *(Pause.)*

EDMOND: Yes. *(Pause.)* Yes, I am. *(Pause.)* Yes.

CHAPLAIN: Why did you kill that girl?

EDMOND: I . . . *(Pause.)* I . . . *(Pause.) I don't* . . . *I* . . . *I don't* . . . *(Pause.)* I . . . *(Pause.)* I don't . . . *(Pause.) I don't* . . . *(Pause.)* I don't think . . . *(Pause.)* I . . . *(Pause.) (The* CHAPLAIN *helps* ED-MOND *up and leads him to the door.)*

Scene Twenty-two.
Alone in the Cell.

EDMOND, *alone in his cell, writes:*

EDMOND: Dear Mrs. Brown. You don't remember me. Perhaps you do. Do you remember Eddie Burke who lived on Euclid? Maybe you do. I took Debbie to the prom. I know that she never found me attractive, and I think, perhaps she was coerced in some way to go with me—though I can't think in what way. It also strikes me as I write that maybe she went of her own free will and I found it important to *think* that she went unwillingly. *(Pause.)* I don't think, however, this is true. *(Pause.)* She was a lovely girl. I'm sure if you remember me you will recall how taken I was with her then.

(A GUARD enters EDMOND's cell.)

GUARD: You have a visitor.

EDMOND: Please tell them that I'm ill.

(GUARD exits. EDMOND gets up. Stretches. Goes to the window. Looks out.)

(To himself) What a day!

(He goes back to his table. Sits down. Yawns. Picks up the paper.)

Scene twenty-three.
In the Prison Cell.

EDMOND *and the* **PRISONER** *are each lying on their bunks.*

EDMOND: You can't control what you make of your life.

PRISONER: Now, thass for *damn* sure.

EDMOND: There is a destiny that shapes our ends. . . .

PRISONER: . . . Uh-huh . . .

EDMOND: Rough-hew them how we may.

PRISONER: How *e'er* we motherfucking may.

EDMOND: And that's the truth.

PRISONER: You *know* that is the truth.

EDMOND: . . . And people say it's *heredity,* or it's environment . . . but, but I think it's something else.

PRISONER: What you think that it is?

EDMOND: I think it's something *beyond* that.

PRISONER: Uh-huh . . .

EDMOND: *Beyond* those things that we can know. *(Pause.)*
I think maybe in dreams we see what it is. *(Pause.)*
What do you think? *(Pause.)*

PRISONER: I don't know.

EDMOND: I don't think we *can* know. I think that if we *knew* it, we'd be dead.

PRISONER: We would be *God*.

EDMOND: We would be God. That's absolutely right.

PRISONER: Or, or some *genius*.

EDMOND: No, I don't think even *genius* could know what it is.

PRISONER: No, some great *genius, (Pause)* or some *philosopher* . . .

EDMOND: I don't think even a *genius* can see what we are.

PRISONER: You don't . . . *think* that . . . *(Pause.)*

EDMOND: I think that we can't perceive it.

PRISONER: Well, *something's* going on, I'll tell you *that.* I'm saying, *somewhere some* poor sucker knows what's happening.

EDMOND: Do you think?

PRISONER: *Shit* yes. Some whacked-out sucker. Somewhere. In the Ozarks? *(Pause.) Shit* yes. Some guy. *(Pause.)* Some *inbred* sucker, walks around all day . . .

(Pause.)

EDMOND: You think?

PRISONER: Yeah. Maybe not *him* . . . but someone. *(Pause.)* Some fuck locked up, he's got time for reflection. . . .

(Pause.)

Or some fuckin' . . . *I* don't know, some *kid,* who's just been *born. (Pause.)*

EDMOND: Some kid that's just been born . . .

PRISONER: Yes. And you know, he's got no preconceptions . . .

EDMOND: Yes.

PRISONER: All he's got . . .

EDMOND: . . . That's absolutely right. . . .

PRISONER: *Huh?* . . .

EDMOND: Yes.

PRISONER: Is . . .

EDMOND: Maybe it's *memory*. . . .

PRISONER: That's what I'm *saying*. That it just may *be*. . . .

EDMOND: It could be.

PRISONER: Or . . .

EDMOND: . . . or some . . .

PRISONER: . . . some . . .

EDMOND: . . . *knowledge* . . .

PRISONER: . . . some . . .

EDMOND: . . . some *intuition*. . . .

PRISONER: Yes.

EDMOND: I don't *even* mean "intuition." . . . Something . . . something . . .

PRISONER: Or some *animal* . . .

EDMOND: Why not? . . .

PRISONER: That all the time we're saying we'll wait for the men from *space*, maybe they're *here*. . . .

EDMOND: . . . Maybe they are. . . .

PRISONER: . . . Maybe they're *animals*. . . .

EDMOND: Yes.

PRISONER: That were *left* here . . .

EDMOND: *Aeons* ago.

PRISONER: *Long* ago . . .

EDMOND: . . . and have *bred* here . . .

PRISONER: Or maybe *we're* the animals. . . .

EDMOND: . . . Maybe we are. . . .

PRISONER: *You* know, how they, *they* are supreme on their . . .

EDMOND: . . . Yes.

PRISONER: On their *native* world . . .

EDMOND: But when you put them here.

PRISONER: *We* say they're only *dogs,* or *animals,* and *scorn* them. . . .

EDMOND: . . . Yes.

PRISONER: We scorn them in our fear. But . . . don't you think? . . .

EDMOND: . . . It very well could be. . . .

PRISONER: But on their native *world* . . .

EDMOND: . . . Uh-huh . . .

PRISONER: . . . they are *supreme.* . . .

EDMOND: I think that's very . . .

PRISONER: And what *we* have done is to disgrace ourselves.

EDMOND: We have.

PRISONER: Because we did not treat them with respeck.

EDMOND *(pause):* Maybe *we* were the animals.

PRISONER: Well, thass what I'm saying.

EDMOND: Maybe they're here to watch over us. Maybe that's why they're here. Or to observe us. Maybe we're here to be punished.

(Pause.)

Do you think there's a Hell?

PRISONER: I don't know. *(Pause.)*

EDMOND: Do you think that we are there?

PRISONER: I don't know, man. *(Pause.)*

EDMOND: Do you think that we go somewhere when we die?

PRISONER: I don't know, man. I *like* to think so.

EDMOND: I would, too.

PRISONER: I sure would like to think so. *(Pause.)*

EDMOND: Perhaps it's Heaven.

PRISONER *(pause):* I don't know.

EDMOND: I don't know either but perhaps it is. *(Pause.)*

PRISONER: I would like to think so.

EDMOND: I would, too.

(Pause.)

Good night. *(Pause.)*

PRISONER: Good night.

(EDMOND *gets up, goes over and exchanges a good-night kiss with the* **PRISONER.** *He then returns to his bed and lies down.)*